THE KIDS' GUIDE
TO
FIGURATIVE
LANGUAGE

A Comprehensive Workbook
for
Upper Elementary Students

Yellow Balloon Press 2024

TABLE OF CONTENTS

HELLO THERE !

HOW TO USE THIS BOOK

OPTION 1: One at a Time

Practice each type of figurative language one at a time. Look at the tracker on page 5 and choose which figurative language you'd like to do first. Work your way through those pages using the tracker as your guide. Mark off the pages you complete on the tracker to keep record of your progress.

OPTION 2: Mix It Up!

Go through each page of the workbook starting with page 13 in numerical order. You will skip around to different types of figurative language as you move through the pages. Use the tracker on page 5 to check off the pages you complete.

WHAT'S INSIDE?

Fill In Fun – Create sentences that include figurative language using the word bank to help you fill in the blanks.

Spot the Figurative Language – Find examples of figurative language in sentences.

Find Your Path – Make your way through a maze by identifying the given type of figurative language.

Write On! – Follow the given prompt to creatively use figurative language in your writing.

Silly Stories – Play with a friend or family member. Person A holds the workbook and asks Person B to think of the type of word listed in the silly story. Without looking at the page, Person B gives their answer, and Person A writes it down in the workbook. When all spaces are filled in, Person A reads the silly story aloud.

Bonus – A fun and unique way to practice.

Review Pages – A mixed review of all you've learned!

TRACK YOUR PROGRESS

Color each box as you complete that page.

SIMILES

page 16	page 23	page 31	page 37	page 45	page 48

METAPHORS

page 13	page 21	page 28	page 34	page 43	page 49

PERSONIFICATION

page 14	page 20	page 22	page 26	page 33	page 50

ALLITERATION

page 15	page 19	page 24	page 36	page 42	page 51

ONOMATOPOEIA

page 17	page 30	page 35	page 39	page 41	page 52

HYPERBOLE

page 25	page 32	page 40	page 44	page 47	page 53

IDIOMS

page 18	page 27	page 29	page 38	page 46	page 54

SIMILES

DEFINITION

a comparison using the words "like" or "as"

EXAMPLES

Carly remained **as stubborn as a mule**, refusing to eat her vegetables.

Tim felt **as brave as a knight facing a dragon** when he stood up to the school bully.

METAPHORS

DEFINITION

a comparison that does NOT use the words "like" or "as"

EXAMPLES

Mrs. Spring is a wise owl, always offering great advice.

Nurse Megan is a gentle lamb to all the sick children she cares for.

PERSONIFICATION

DEFINITION

giving human characteristics to a nonhuman thing

EXAMPLES

The wind whispered through the trees.

The sun sank down in the valley as the mountains stood guard over the village.

ALLITERATION

DEFINITION

using the same sound multiple times

EXAMPLES

The group of girls gathered to greet Gretchen.

My mom makes the most marvelous muffins.

ONOMATOPOEIA

DEFINITION

a word that sounds like the sound it makes

EXAMPLES

I heard the balloon **pop** when it hit the tree.

The **crash** of the cymbals told us the parade was about to begin.

HYPERBOLE

DEFINITION

a large exaggeration

EXAMPLES

I have **a million hours** of homework tonight!

It took **forever** to go through the lunch line.

IDIOMS

DEFINITION

a phrase that means something different than its literal meaning

EXAMPLES

I had **butterflies in my stomach** before the Spelling Bee.

It's raining cats and dogs out there!

Fill In Fun

Directions: Use the word bank to help you fill in the blanks to create metaphors.

Word Bank				
room	city	key	paint	storm
thief	magic	hug	diamonds	sponge

1. The future is a blank canvas, waiting for us to _____ our dreams on it.

2. The _____ was a bustling beehive of activity.

3. Jared's anger is a _____ brewing on the horizon.

4. Time is a _____ that steals away moments when we're having fun.

5. Brady's _____ was a disaster zone, with clothes thrown everywhere.

6. Love is a warm _____ on a cold day.

7. The stars are tiny _____ scattered across the night sky.

8. Daniel's mind is a _____, absorbing knowledge everywhere he goes.

9. Books are _____ carpets that transport us to different worlds.

10. Curiosity is the _____ that unlocks the door to knowledge.

13

© Tracy Sievers 2024

Find Your Path

Directions: Read the sentence in each box. If it's an example of personification, color it your favorite color. If it's not, leave it blank. If you do it correctly, you will create a colored path from the START box to the END box that ONLY contains examples of personification.

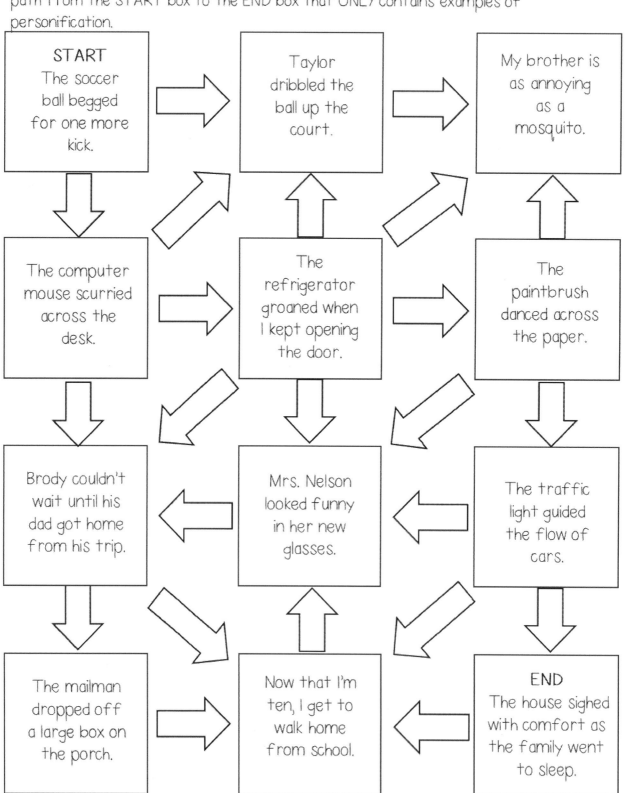

START The soccer ball begged for one more kick.

Taylor dribbled the ball up the court.

My brother is as annoying as a mosquito.

The computer mouse scurried across the desk.

The refrigerator groaned when I kept opening the door.

The paintbrush danced across the paper.

Brody couldn't wait until his dad got home from his trip.

Mrs. Nelson looked funny in her new glasses.

The traffic light guided the flow of cars.

The mailman dropped off a large box on the porch.

Now that I'm ten, I get to walk home from school.

END The house sighed with comfort as the family went to sleep.

14

☺ Silly Alliteration Story ☺

In the heart of the _____ , young Tate tiptoed
place
through the towering trees, his tiny toes tingling with
each step. He trailed through the terrain, tracing
tracks of tiny creatures and _____ at the
past tense verb
twinkling snowflakes that _____ on the
past tense verb
ground. With each breath, Tate tasted the crispness
of the air. He could smell the tantalizing scent of
_____ and _____ . As Tate trekked deeper
scent   _scent_
into the wilderness, he heard a _____ tapping
adjective
overhead. Looking up, he _____ a trio of
past tense verb
_____ , their tiny bodies trembling with the
plural animal
chill as they searched the frozen _____ looking for
thing
hidden treasures. Tate watched the _____
adjective
animals brave the cold. Suddenly, his attention turned
to a towering tree, its trunk twisted and tangled like a
tale from a _____ . With a twinkle in his
thing
_____ and a tug at his _____ , Tate began to
body part   _piece of clothing_
climb. At the top, he turned and took in the
_____ view, the entire tundra stretching
adjective
out before him. With a sigh, Tate _____ onto
past tense verb
a branch, feeling truly at home in this _____ ,
adjective
snowy wonderland.

# Write On!

Directions: Imagine you could shrink down to the size of a bug for a day. Describe your miniature adventure. Use at least **THREE SIMILES** in your story. Underline them.

_____

_____

_____

_____

_____

_____

_____

_____

_____

_____

_____

_____

👀 Spot the Onomatopoeia 👀

Directions: Read the sentences below. Underline the example of onomatopoeia in each one.

1. The tires screech as the car comes to a sudden stop.

2. The duck quacks loudly by the pond, chatting with its feathered friends.

3. Every time someone walks by, my dog barks loudly.

4. The scent of popcorn fills the room as it pops in the microwave.

5. As I step on the ice, I hear it crack beneath my feet.

6. The pig oinks happily in the mud, enjoying its bath.

7. The colorful leaves rustle in the gentle breeze.

8. I was woken up to the thud of my brother slamming his door.

9. The hum of the fan helped me drift off to sleep.

10. The ice cubes clink in the glass as Crista pours the soda.

Find Your Path

Directions: Read the sentences in each box. If it is an idiom, color it your favorite color. If it's not, leave it blank. If you do it correctly, you will create a colored path from the START box to the END box that ONLY contains examples of idioms.

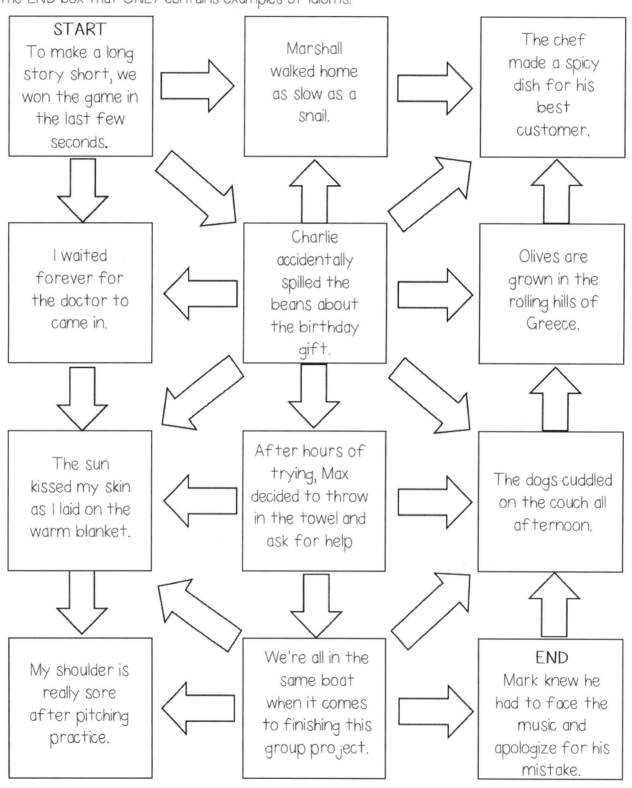

START
To make a long story short, we won the game in the last few seconds.

Marshall walked home as slow as a snail.

The chef made a spicy dish for his best customer.

I waited forever for the doctor to came in.

Charlie accidentally spilled the beans about the birthday gift.

Olives are grown in the rolling hills of Greece.

The sun kissed my skin as I laid on the warm blanket.

After hours of trying, Max decided to throw in the towel and ask for help

The dogs cuddled on the couch all afternoon.

My shoulder is really sore after pitching practice.

We're all in the same boat when it comes to finishing this group project.

END
Mark knew he had to face the music and apologize for his mistake.

18

Fill In Fun

Directions: Use the word bank to help you fill in the blanks to create examples of alliteration.

Word Bank				
wisdom	kite	tiptoed	children	Natalie
monkey	diary	battled	pink	scampered

1. Beneath the big, bustling bridge, bugs _____ for bits of bread.

2. Katie the kind-hearted kid kept a keen eye on her _____.

3. Wally the wizard waved his wand, whispering words of _____ to a wandering wolf.

4. Cheery _____ chased chubby chipmunks, chuckling in the cherry orchard.

5. _____ noticed noisy neighborhood birds nesting near her new nectarine tree.

6. Silly squirrels _____ swiftly, searching for snacks.

7. Molly the mischievous _____ made marvelous mud pies.

8. Penny the pirate painted pictures of _____ parrots and pirate ships.

9. Dr. Doodle drew dazzling dragons in his dusty old _____.

10. Terrific tigers _____ through the tangled trees.

☺ Silly Personification Story ☺

Kia was so excited to finally go to the beach. She and her friend, _____ (person's name), had been planning this trip for as long as she could remember. As the girls stepped onto the beach, Kia couldn't help but notice the beautiful _____ (color) and _____ (color) of the morning sky. The sun stretched its warm rays to greet them, as they spread their _____ (things) out and put on sunscreen. The _____ (adjective) sand sighed with relief, eager to feel their playful footsteps. The girls _____ (past tense verb) into the water, feeling it embrace them like a refreshing hug. Kia _____ (past tense verb) as the waves danced towards her, their foamy fingers tickling her toes like _____ (person) used to do when she was little. After _____ (number) minutes of _____ (verb + ing) in the waves, the girls began to get hungry. They _____ (past tense verb) back to their towels and searched their bags for a snack. They settled on some _____ (food) and _____ (food). _____ (plural animal) soared overhead, watching to see if they would _____ (verb) any crumbs. As they sat on the sand, Kia wouldn't help but smile. She was in her favorite place with her very _____ (adjective ending with "est") friend. And when she _____ (past tense verb) at the ocean in front of her, the water smiled right back.

20

⇨ Find Your Path ⇦

Directions: Read the sentences in each box. If it is a metaphor, color it your favorite color. If it's not, leave it blank. If you do it correctly, you will create a colored path from the START box to the END box that ONLY contains examples of metaphors.

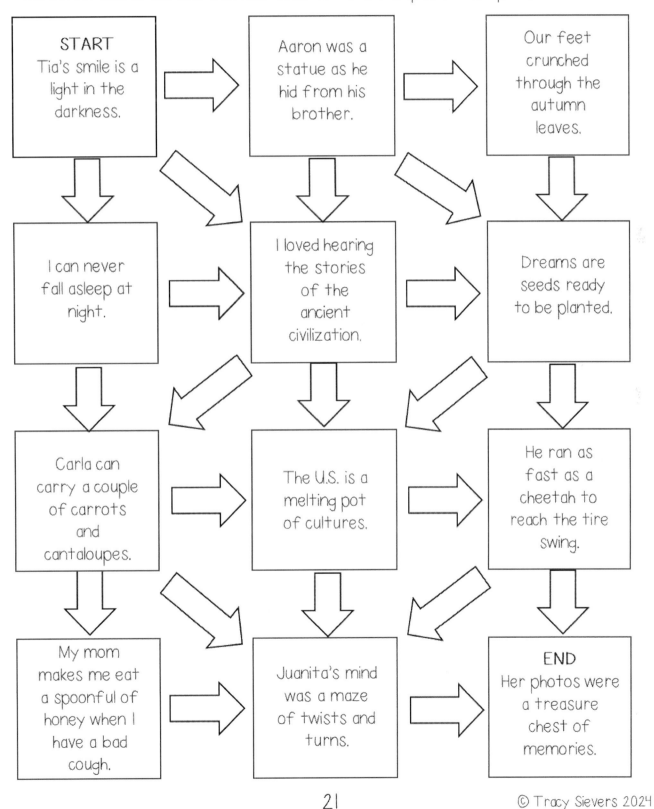

START
Tia's smile is a light in the darkness.

Aaron was a statue as he hid from his brother.

Our feet crunched through the autumn leaves.

I can never fall asleep at night.

I loved hearing the stories of the ancient civilization.

Dreams are seeds ready to be planted.

Carla can carry a couple of carrots and cantaloupes.

The U.S. is a melting pot of cultures.

He ran as fast as a cheetah to reach the tire swing.

My mom makes me eat a spoonful of honey when I have a bad cough.

Juanita's mind was a maze of twists and turns.

END
Her photos were a treasure chest of memories.

21

 Fill In Fun

Directions: Use the word bank to help you fill in the blanks to create sentences that use personification.

Word Bank				
arms	walked	page	groaned	ink
clock	road	hugged	clouds	wind

1. The _____ whispered secrets through the trees.

2. The pencil raced across the _____, eager to tell a story.

3. The stairs _____ under our weight

4. The shadows chased us as we _____.

5. The _____ screamed at us to wake up.

6. The tree branches reached out like welcoming _____.

7. The _____ played hide and seek with the sun.

8. The dirt _____ stretched out before us.

9. The pen refused to cooperate, running out of _____.

10. The blanket _____ us to keep us warm.

👀 Spot the Simile 👀

Directions: Read the sentences below. Underline the simile in each one.

1. Deanna's eyes sparkled like diamonds in the early morning sunlight.

2. The raindrops fell from the sky like tiny dancers leaping across the stage.

3. Mr. Cane's voice was as loud as thunder during a storm.

4. The bird's song was as sweet as a lullaby.

5. The mountain stood tall and strong like a giant.

6. The baby's cheeks were as pink as cotton candy.

7. The flowers in the garden bloomed like colorful fireworks.

8. The snowflakes fell from the sky as gently as feathers.

9. Ann's blonde hair flowed behind her like a golden river.

10. The rainbow stretched across the sky like a colorful bridge.

23

 Write On!

Directions: Write a story about a young inventor who builds a robot companion out of spare parts. What adventures do they go on together? Choose a letter of the alphabet. Use at least **TEN words** that start with that letter to make your story **ALLITERATIVE.** Underline those words.

_____

_____

_____

_____

_____

_____

_____

_____

_____

_____

_____

_____

Find Your Path

Directions: Read the sentences in each box. If it's an example of a hyperbole, color it your favorite color. If it's not, leave it blank. If you do it correctly, you will create a colored path from the START box to the END box that ONLY contains examples of hyperbole.

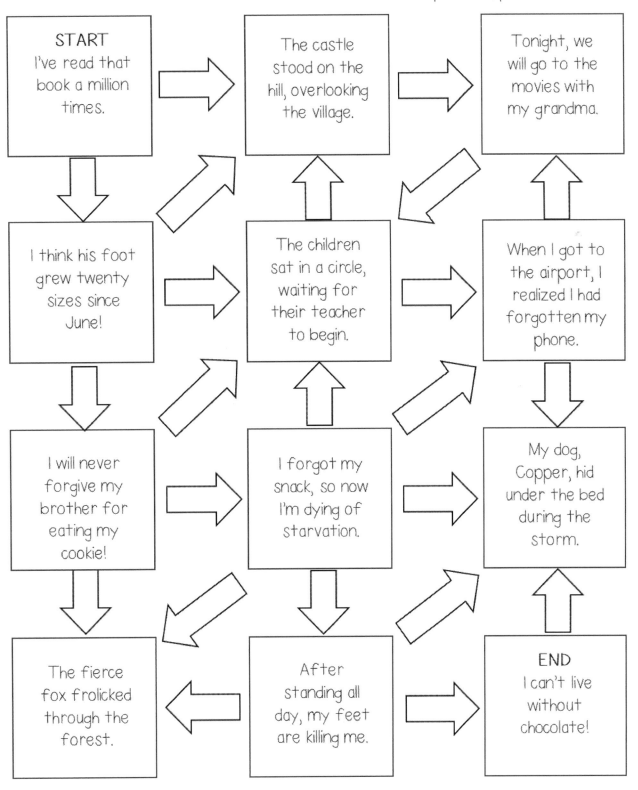

START
I've read that book a million times.

The castle stood on the hill, overlooking the village.

Tonight, we will go to the movies with my grandma.

I think his foot grew twenty sizes since June!

The children sat in a circle, waiting for their teacher to begin.

When I got to the airport, I realized I had forgotten my phone.

I will never forgive my brother for eating my cookie!

I forgot my snack, so now I'm dying of starvation.

My dog, Copper, hid under the bed during the storm.

The fierce fox frolicked through the forest.

After standing all day, my feet are killing me.

END
I can't live without chocolate!

👀 Spot the Personification 👀

1. The backpack slouched under the weight of the books.

2. The haunted house patiently waited for the children to enter.

3. The stars winked at us from the night sky.

4. The leaves waved goodbye as they fell from the trees.

5. As the river flowed, it sang a gentle lullaby.

6. The thunder growled angrily in the distance.

7. The flashlight guarded us in the darkness.

8. The recess whistle demanded the attention of the students.

9. The gooey pizza called out to be eaten.

10. The roller coaster screamed as it came to a stop.

☺ Silly Idiom Story ☺

In the town of _____, there lived a boy named Gabriel.
                    city
Gabriel was a _____ student, but he had a big test
                 adjective
coming up that was making him feel like a fish out of
water. He had studied hard for weeks, but the night before
the test, he realized he had left his notes at _____.
                                                    place
Gabriel's heart sank, fearing he'd be in trouble because he
hadn't hit the books as he should have. He knew he had to
face the music and do his best. As Gabriel _____
                                              past tense verb
into the classroom, he saw his classmates chatting and
_____. _____ handed out the
  verb + ing   *person*
_____, and Gabriel's anxiety grew. He wished he could
 plural thing
turn back time and _____ harder, but it was too late.
                        verb
Taking a deep breath, he resolved to go the extra mile and
rely on what he could remember. As Gabriel _____
                                               past tense verb
through the test, he couldn't help but worry. But he was
determined not to throw in the towel, even if things
seemed _____. Suddenly, he recalled something his
         adjective
mom always said: "Don't count your chickens before they
hatch." He realized he couldn't let his nerves get the best of
him. With determination, he kept working, answering each
question to the best of his ability. Finally, the _____
                                                      thing
rang, signaling the end of the test. Gabriel felt a
_____ sense of relief. Whether he passed or failed,
 adjective
he knew that he'd be sure to be prepared for his next
test so that it would be a piece of cake!

27

⚷ Write On! ⚷

Directions: You discover a key that opens a secret door in your school. Where does it lead? Describe what you find. Use at least THREE METAPHORS in your story. Underline them.

_____

_____

_____

_____

_____

_____

_____

_____

_____

_____

_____

_____

Fill In Fun

Directions: Use the word bank to help you fill in the blanks to create idioms.

Word Bank				
hit	ice	bag	biting	pigs
cake	around	nail	raining	bucket

1. That test was a piece of _____!

2. Making a joke helped me break the _____ with my new classmates.

3. Sarah really hit the _____ on the head when she guessed my favorite color.

4. Don't let the cat out of the _____ about the surprise party!

5. My mom said I could get a pony for my birthday when _____ fly.

6. I wanted to join the soccer team, but I'm so busy that I might be _____ off more than I can chew.

7. It's not just a light drizzle, it's _____ cats and dogs out there!

8. Stop beating _____ the bush and just tell me what happened.

9. I hope to travel the world before I kick the _____.

10. After a long day, I'm ready to _____ the hay.

Find Your Path

Directions: Read the sentences in each box. If it is an example of onomatopoeia, color it your favorite color. If it's not, leave it blank. If you do it correctly, you will create a colored path from the START box to the END box that ONLY contains examples of onomatopoeia.

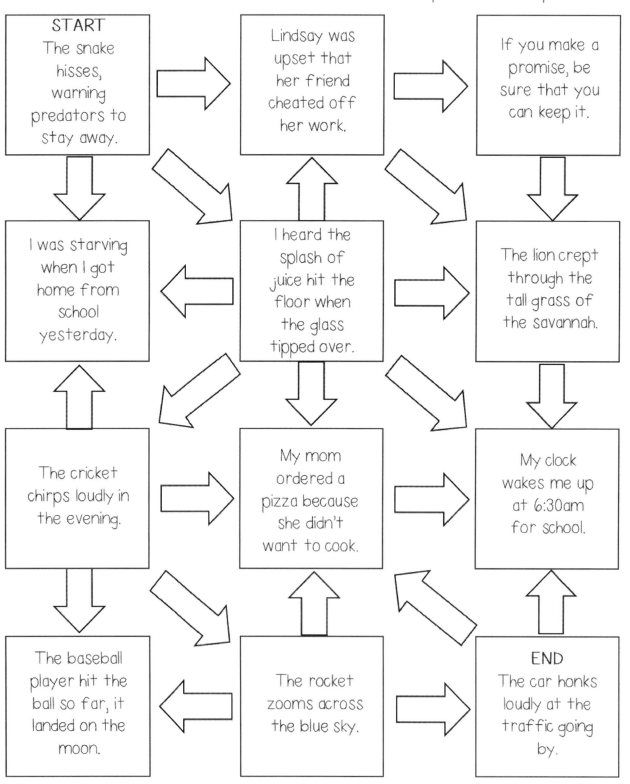

START
The snake hisses, warning predators to stay away.

Lindsay was upset that her friend cheated off her work.

If you make a promise, be sure that you can keep it.

I was starving when I got home from school yesterday.

I heard the splash of juice hit the floor when the glass tipped over.

The lion crept through the tall grass of the savannah.

The cricket chirps loudly in the evening.

My mom ordered a pizza because she didn't want to cook.

My clock wakes me up at 6:30am for school.

The baseball player hit the ball so far, it landed on the moon.

The rocket zooms across the blue sky.

END
The car honks loudly at the traffic going by.

30

Fill In Fun

Directions: Use the word bank to help you fill in the blanks to create similes.

Word Bank				
zoomed	popped	wand	bird	curiosity
air	honey	twinkled	slithering	tears

1. Her _____ fell like silent raindrops on a windowpane.

2. The silence hung in the _____ like a heavy cloud.

3. His _____ bubbled up inside him like a fizzy soda

4. The basketball player soared through the air like a _____ taking flight.

5. The campfire crackled and _____ like a bowl of popcorn

6. The stars _____ above like a host of fireflies in the night sky.

7. The car _____ down the road as fast as a shooting star.

8. The paintbrush danced across the canvas like a magician's _____.

9. The roller coaster twisted and turned like a snake _____ through the air.

10. The cookie was as sweet as _____ dripping from a hive.

☺ Silly Hyperbole Story ☺

Caleb and Mia loved going on adventures. One _____
                                                    adjective
morning, they decided to explore the mystical Cave of
Echoes, rumored to be a million times larger than any other
cave in the area. Caleb's mom packed a _____
                                               thing
for them to take and filled it with tons of snacks...
including her homemade chocolate chip _____...
                                              plural food
which everyone agreed were the best in the universe.
Armed with their trusty backpacks filled with snacks that
weighed a ton, they _____ on their quest. The
                      past tense verb
journey to the cave took forever. When they finally got
there, they stared up at the _____ entrance. As
                                   adjective
they ventured into the cave, the air grew so quiet they
could hear a pin drop. But Caleb and Mia weren't scared.
They were _____! After an hour, Caleb stopped to
            emotion
get a snack. "I'm starving!" he said as he sat on a
_____, eating a _____. After a short break,
    thing   food
the friends began walking again, being careful not to slip on
the _____ rocks. Suddenly, they could see lights
        adjective
reflecting up ahead. The kids _____ towards it and
                                 past tense verb
happened upon a _____ cavern filled with gems the
                     adjective
size of boulders. "_____!" exclaimed Mia, her eyes
                       exclamation
widening in awe. Caleb agreed, imagining what he could buy
with all this treasure. The two friends _____ at
                                            past tense verb
each other, barely able to believe their luck.

32

 Write On!

Directions: Think about your dream bedroom. What would be in it? How would it look? Describe it in detail. Use at least THREE examples of PERSONIFICATION in your writing. Underline them.

_____

_____

_____

_____

_____

_____

_____

_____

_____

_____

_____

☺ Silly Metaphor Story ☺

_____ year old Jack was always up for an adventure,
number
especially if it took place outdoors. So, when his grandpa
suggested a camping trip, Jack didn't hesitate to say
_____. He spent the week collecting everything he thought
exclamation
he may need for his adventure. The day finally _____, and
past tense verb
his grandpa picked him up, ready to begin their weekend together.
They pulled their _____ into the parking lot of the
thing
_____, gathered their supplies, and headed deep into
place
the woods. As they came to a small clearing, Jack spotted a
kaleidoscope of flowers surrounding him. The colors were
_____! They continued to _____ until they came upon
adjective   *verb*
a _____ spot next to a _____ creek. It was the
adjective   *adjective*
perfect place to set up camp. Jack and his grandpa _____
adverb
pitched their tent and started a crackling fire. The flames were
a thick blanket, _____ them up despite the chill in the air.
verb + ing
They sat together, sharing stories and eating _____ s'mores
adjective
packed with extra _____. Jack started to get
food
_____, so they decided to head to bed. The moon shone
feeling
in the sky, a lantern guiding them back to their tent. Jack felt
happy and safe as he crawled into his _____ sleeping bag,
adjective
ready for a night under the _____ with his grandpa by his
plural noun
side. The sound of the crickets chirping was a soothing lullaby for
Jack and his grandpa as they drifted to sleep. Jack _____
past tense verb
with a smile on his face, _____ about the new adventures
verb + ing
they'd go on the next day.

34

Fill In Fun

Directions: Use the word bank to help you fill in the blanks to create onomatopoeia.

Word Bank				
crackles	hooves	rumbles	clock	whooshes
pan	buzz	meows	birds	rain

1. The bees _____ around the flowers, gathering nectar.

2. The tick tock of the _____ counts down the minutes until recess.

3. The thunder _____ loudly, like a giant's belly at dinnertime.

4. The _____ pitter-patters on the roof, making it hard to hear what my mom is saying.

5. The horse's _____ clippity-clop along the cobblestone street.

6. The fire _____ in the fireplace as we snuggle on the couch.

7. The cat _____ loudly outside the door when he wants to come in.

8. The _____ chirp cheerfully in the morning, singing a wake-up song.

9. The wind _____ through the trees, like a superhero rushing by.

10. The _____ sizzles as the bacon cooks in the skillet.

👀 Spot the Alliteration 👀

1. Fiona the fearless fairy flew through the forest, fluttering her feathery wings.

2. Gabe and Greta gobbled yummy gummy bears.

3. Hannah happily hummed her favorite tunes while hiking through the heavenly hills.

4. In July, Jake and Jenny joyfully drove to the jamboree.

5. Little Lucy listened to the lullabies of the lazy, lapping waves.

6. Ruby the rabbit raced rapidly around the wet, rocky road.

7. Swiftly sliding down snowy slopes, round snowmen sang silly songs .

8. Curious cats cuddled together, watching the colorful caterpillars .

9. Daring Danny delightfully darted down the orange slide.

10. Busy bees buzzed in the budding blossoms.

Find Your Path

Directions: Read the sentences in each box. If it is a simile, color it your favorite color. If it's not, leave it blank. If you do it correctly, you will create a colored path from the START box to the END box that ONLY contains examples of similes.

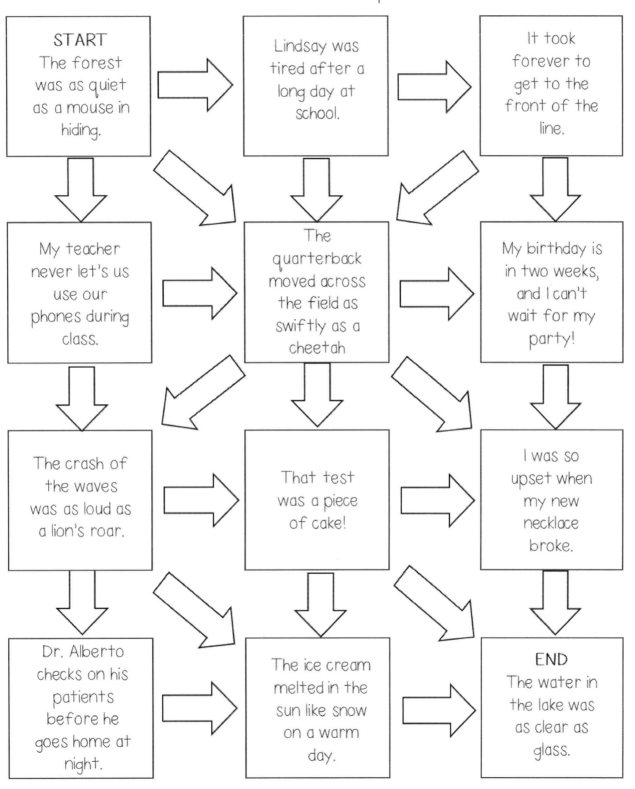

START The forest was as quiet as a mouse in hiding.

Lindsay was tired after a long day at school.

It took forever to get to the front of the line.

My teacher never let's us use our phones during class.

The quarterback moved across the field as swiftly as a cheetah

My birthday is in two weeks, and I can't wait for my party!

The crash of the waves was as loud as a lion's roar.

That test was a piece of cake!

I was so upset when my new necklace broke.

Dr. Alberto checks on his patients before he goes home at night.

The ice cream melted in the sun like snow on a warm day.

END The water in the lake was as clear as glass.

37

👀 Spot the Idiom 👀

Directions: Read the sentences below. Underline the idiom in each one.

1. Tell me all about your day, I'm all ears.

2. Don't worry about the test next week. Let's cross that bridge when we get to it.

3. Be sure to sign up for a few classes so you don't put all your eggs in one basket.

4. My grandma came to visit out of the blue.

5. Right before the Spelling Bee I had butterflies in my stomach.

6. Don't celebrate until the game is over because we don't want to count our chickens before they hatch.

7. I got my chores done by 9:00am because the early bird catches the worm.

8. There's no need to make a mountain out of a molehill.

9. The new girl hoped her classmates wouldn't judge a book by its cover.

10. When Sandra got caught in a lie, she found herself in a pickle.

☺ Silly Onomatopoeia Story ☺

Lyla had been counting down the days until her eleventh birthday. The morning of her big day, she woke up to the sound of birds tweeting happily outside her _____ .
                                                                                      thing
She _____ out of bed, eager to start her day.
        past tense verb
Downstairs in the _____ , her mom was already busy
                        name of room
preparing a _____ breakfast. The scent of
                adjective
_____ filled the air, accompanied by the sizzle of
    food
_____ as her mom expertly stood at the stove. Lyla's
    food
stomach rumbled with hunger as she eagerly awaited her birthday feast. After breakfast, she heard a bang at the front door. Her friends were arriving for her party! The
girls _____ to the backyard to hang out. Lyla's mom
        past tense verb
carried the balloons and the cake outside as the girls played. Suddenly, there was a large pop, causing everyone to
_____ in surprise. The girls burst into giggles when
    verb
they realized it was just Lyla's little brother playing with a
_____ . As the day went on, Lyla's mom said it was
time to do the _____-shaped pinata. Lyla's friends each had
    thing   *thing*
a turn trying to hit it. As Lyla swung the stick, a loud crack
                            thing
sounded, and _____ flew all over the ground. When it was
                things
finally time for cake, Lyla closed her eyes and made a wish
before blowing out the _____ candles. She felt so lucky to
                            number
have so many _____ friends. This was a birthday
                    adjective
she would never forget.

39

 Fill In Fun

Directions: Use the word bank to help you fill in the blanks to create examples of hyperbole.

Word Bank				
wake	brain	lightning	skyscraper	homework
waited	universe	suitcase	sleep	million

1. Kaitlyn grew taller than a _____ last summer.

2. I've told you a _____ times to clean your room.

3. His snoring is so loud, it could _____ the dead.

4. I can't carry my _____ because it weighs a ton!

5. I'm so tired today, I could _____ for a week.

6. My grandma makes the best cookies in the entire _____.

7. I've got a mountain of _____ to do tonight.

8. I'm pretty sure my brother's _____ is the size of a pea.

9. I _____ in line for ages to get tickets for the concert.

10. Nevaeh is faster than _____ on the basketball court.

 Write On!

Directions: Write a diary entry from the perspective of a pirate sailing across the sea. Use at least **FOUR examples of ONOMATOPOEIA** in your story. Underline them.

_____

_____

_____

_____

_____

_____

_____

_____

_____

_____

_____

_____

 Find Your Path

Directions: Read the sentence in each box. If it is an example of alliteration, color it your favorite color. If it's not, leave it blank. If you do it correctly, you will create a colored path from the START box to the END box that ONLY contains examples of alliteration.

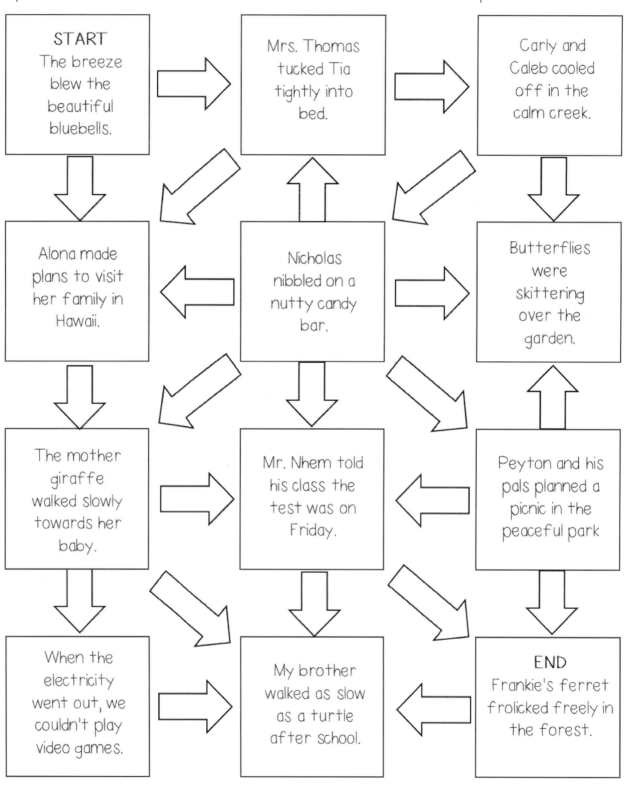

START
The breeze blew the beautiful bluebells.

Mrs. Thomas tucked Tia tightly into bed.

Carly and Caleb cooled off in the calm creek.

Alona made plans to visit her family in Hawaii.

Nicholas nibbled on a nutty candy bar.

Butterflies were skittering over the garden.

The mother giraffe walked slowly towards her baby.

Mr. Nhem told his class the test was on Friday.

Peyton and his pals planned a picnic in the peaceful park

When the electricity went out, we couldn't play video games.

My brother walked as slow as a turtle after school.

END
Frankie's ferret frolicked freely in the forest.

42

👀 Spot the Metaphor 👀

Directions: Read the sentences below. Underline the metaphor in each one.

1. The ocean is a giant, blue blanket stretching to the horizon.

2. Problems are puzzles, waiting to be solved.

3. The road to success is a winding path with many twists and turns.

4. Eva's dream was the spark that ignited her creativity.

5. Forgiveness is a bridge that mends broken hearts.

6. My brother is a squirrel, always scurrying around.

7. Chloe's smile is a ray of sunshine on a rainy day.

8. Mr. Wooten's words were a sword that cut through the silence.

9. The world is a playground full of adventures waiting to happen.

10. The moon is a silver coin in the dark sky.

 Write On!

Directions: Write a story about a group of animals in a city who band together to solve mysteries and protect their neighborhood. Use at least THREE examples of HYPERBOLE in your story. Underline them.

_____

_____

_____

_____

_____

_____

_____

_____

_____

_____

_____

☺ Silly Simile Story ☺

It was the first day of school in _____. Lily
was in fourth grade this year and was so
_____ for school to begin. Carrying her
trusty _____, she walked through the
_____ of her school. Her teacher,
_____, greeted her with a smile as
warm as the _____. As Lily walked to her
desk, her best friend, _____, came in. Lily
couldn't believe it. They had been in the same class
for the last _____ years! She felt as
_____ as a four-leaf clover. Lily sat
down and started _____ her school
supplies. She loved having all new stuff! She put
her stack of notebooks in her desk and pulled out
a perfectly pointed _____. The bell rang, and
everyone settled into their seats. It suddenly got
as quiet as a _____. Lily looked over at
her best friend and got the feeling this was going
to be a _____ school year!

(labels under blanks: city, emotion, thing, plural noun, famous person, thing, name, number, adjective, verb + ing, thing, animal, adjective)

45

Write On!

Directions: You wake up one morning to find that your pet has learned to speak! Describe what happens. Use at least **THREE IDIOMS** in your story. Underline them.

👀 Spot the Hyperbole 👀

Directions: Read the sentences below. Underline the hyperbole example in each one.

1. I have a billion things on my mind right now.

2. My mom is blind without her glasses.

3. My backpack is bursting at the seams with books.

4. The party was louder than a rock concert.

5. I've been studying for so long that my brain is mushy.

6. The traffic jam was so long that I thought I'd never get home.

7. The price of gas is sky-high!

8. My mom's to-do list is never-ending.

9. I have looked everywhere for my keys.

10. Knox was so hungry, he felt like he could eat fifty cheeseburgers.

BONUS: I Am Simile Poem

I am...

as sweet as _____.

as funny as _____.

as smart as _____.

as creative as _____.

as playful as _____.

as tired as _____.

as crazy as _____.

as hungry as _____.

as helpful as _____.

as tall as _____.

as excited as _____.

as cuddly as _____.

as strong as _____.

as artistic as _____.

as gentle as _____.

as kind as _____.

as confident as _____.

as hardworking as _____.

as calm as _____.

BONUS: Metaphor Maker

Directions: Create a metaphor by filling in the blanks in the sentences below.

1. Jared was a _____ at recess while he played soccer.

2. Knowledge is a _____ that guides us through hard times.

3. Love is a _____, where patience and care grow.

4. Sheila's anger was a _____, waiting to blow.

5. The classroom was a _____ as the students waited to go on the field trip.

6. My mom was my _____ when I was upset about not making the cheerleading squad.

7. The playground is a _____ full of kids swinging, running, and playing.

8. Lying on the sand, the sun was a _____, warming my skin.

9. Mrs. Morton was a _____, full of knowledge to share.

10. A book is a _____ to another world.

49

BONUS: Pick the Personification

Directions: Read the sentences below. Circle the word in parenthesis that will create an example of personification.

1. The mischievous wind gently (danced/blew) through the trees.

2. The sun (shone/smiled) down on the playground, warming the swings and slides.

3. The car engine (coughed/sputtered) as it struggled to start on the chilly morning.

4. The blanket snugly (hugged/wrapped around) Amanda, keeping her warm at her brother's football game.

5. The clock on the wall (ticked away/counted down) the seconds until recess would start.

6. The floor of the old house (groaned/creaked) as the family walked down the hall.

7. The stars (winked/sparkled) in the sky as we laid in the grass.

8. The thunder crashed (angrily/loudly), shaking the earth..

9. As we sat at the campsite, the moon (peeked out/glowed) from behind the clouds.

10. The raindrops (fell/tap-danced) on the roof of the school.

BONUS: Amazing Alliteration

Directions: Read the prompt. Choose a letter of the alphabet and create an alliterative sentence with at least four examples of alliteration.

EXAMPLE: A monkey eating
The marvelous monkey munched mangos with his mother.

1. A boy at the ocean

_____

_____

2. Dad is driving

_____

_____

3. Tall buildings in the city

_____

_____

4. Grandma's yummy food

_____

_____

5. Kids at the park

_____

_____

BONUS: Onomatopoeia Matching

Directions: Match the example of onomatopoeia on the left with the object that makes that sound on the right.

flutter	electricity
tick tock	cymbals
vroom	car horn
zap	bacon
clink	clock
beep	wind
crash	wings
boom	bee
hiss	ice cubes in a glass
sizzle	water
whoosh	fireworks
buzz	snake
drip	engine

BONUS: Match the Hyperbole

Directions: Match the hyperbole on the left to its meaning on the right.

1. I waited forever for my turn. _____

2. My backpack weighed a ton! _____

3. My teacher gave us ten hours of homework. _____

4. We ran a marathon on P.E. _____

5. I'm starving! I could eat an elephant. _____

6. It was so cold outside that my toes froze on my walk home. _____

7. My dog runs faster than a fighter jet. _____

8. I was too nervous to go down the waterslide because it was taller than a skyscraper. _____

9. I'm so tired I could sleep for a hundred years. _____

10. After working on our project, it looked like a tornado hit our classroom. _____

A. he's fast

B. I'm really sleepy

C. the temperature was low

D. it was messy

E. I'm very hungry

F. I had a lot to do

G. the wait was long

H. it was heavy

I. we ran a long distance

J. it was very tall

BONUS: Draw the Idiom!

Directions: Read the idioms. Draw two versions of it. The first one will be its LITERAL meaning and the second one will be its FIGURATIVE meaning. Have fun!

1. It's **raining cats and dogs** outside!

LITERAL	FIGURATIVE

2. That test was **a piece of cake**!

LITERAL	FIGURATIVE

3. To **break the ice**, the teacher had the students sit on the rug for circle time.

LITERAL	FIGURATIVE

54

TIME FOR A REVIEW

Everything you've learned about figurative language is here in a quick review to really see how much you've learned!

You've got this!

Simile: a comparison using the words "like" or "as"

Metaphor: a comparison that does NOT use the words "like" or "as"

Personification: giving human characteristics to a nonhuman thing

Alliteration: using the same sound multiple times

Onomatopoeia: a word that sounds like the sound it makes

Hyperbole: a large exaggeration

Idiom: a phrase that means something different than its literal meaning

Name It!

1. After the long soccer game, Joy's legs felt as heavy as lead weights.

1. _____

2. The thunderstorm boomed and rumbled overhead, making me jump with each loud clap.

2. _____

3. The heavy backpack was an anchor, weighing down Leroy's shoulders as he trudged home from school.

3. _____

4. Jenna was so excited for her birthday party that she was on cloud nine all week.

4. _____

5. The fluffy white clouds in the sky looked as soft as cotton balls.

5. _____

6. Sahir's sweet, sticky syrup spread slowly over his stack of pancakes.

6. _____

7. Lily was a shining star on the dance floor, her movements graceful and mesmerizing.

7. _____

8. Mom gave me a million reminders to clean my room.

8. _____

9. The chocolate cake winked at me from the kitchen counter, tempting me with its rich frosting.

9. _____

10. Furry forest friends frolicked through the fallen fall leaves.

10. _____

Fill In Fun 2.0

Directions: Notice the type of figurative language in parenthesis before each of the sentences written below. Read the sentence and fill in the blank so that it makes sense.

simile   1. The baby's scream was as loud as a _____.

metaphor   2. The night sky was a _____, twinkling down on the valley.

hyperbole   3. This _____ weighs a ton!

personification   4. The raindrops _____ in the puddles, splashing in the afternoon sun.

alliteration   5. The bouncy, _____ ball bobbed across Ben's bright blue _____.

onomatopoeia   6. The puppy's _____ thumped excitedly against the floor when I gave him a treat.

idiom   7. After hours of begging, mom finally gave Lucy the green light to _____.

simile   8. The ice cream sundae was as tall as a _____, with scoops of ice cream and toppings piled high.

metaphor   9. The _____ was a puzzle that Jake struggled to solve.

hyperbole   10. My dad's snoring could have woken _____ last night.

personification   11. The old _____ groaned with effort as it climbed the steep hill.

alliteration   12. _____, crunchy _____ crackled between Chloe's teeth.

onomatopoeia   13. The bees _____ busily as they gathered nectar from the colorful flowers.

Idiom   14. After a terrible tryout, Jameson felt like he had two left feet when it came to _____.

Figurative Facts

Directions: Think about what you've learned about figurative language. Read each sentence below and decide if it's true or false. Then write your answer on the line to the right.

1. Hyperboles must be realistic descriptions.

1. _____

2. Figurative language can be used to make writing more interesting.

2. _____

3. Onomatopoeia is when words imitate the sounds they describe.

3. _____

4. A simile uses "like" or "as" to compare two things.

4. _____

5. You must use a letter ten times in a sentence for it to be considered alliteration.

5. _____

6. Idioms would be difficult to understand if English wasn't your first language.

6. _____

7. Hyperboles can make things sound bigger or smaller than they really are.

7. _____

8. Personification gives human traits to non-human things.

8. _____

9. You can only use onomatopoeia for animal sounds.

9. _____

10. Similes and metaphors are the same thing.

10. _____

ANSWER KEYS

Fill In Fun Answer Key

Word Bank				
room	city	key	paint	storm
thief	magic	hug	diamonds	sponge

1. The future is a blank canvas, waiting for us to paint our dreams on it.

2. The city was a bustling beehive of activity.

3. Jared's anger is a storm brewing on the horizon.

4. Time is a thief that steals away moments when we're having fun.

5. Brady's room was a disaster zone, with clothes thrown everywhere.

6. Love is a warm hug on a cold day.

7. The stars are tiny diamonds scattered across the night sky.

8. Daniel's mind is a sponge, absorbing knowledge everywhere he goes.

9. Books are magic carpets that transport us to different worlds.

10. Curiosity is the key that unlocks the door to knowledge.

Find Your Path Answer Key

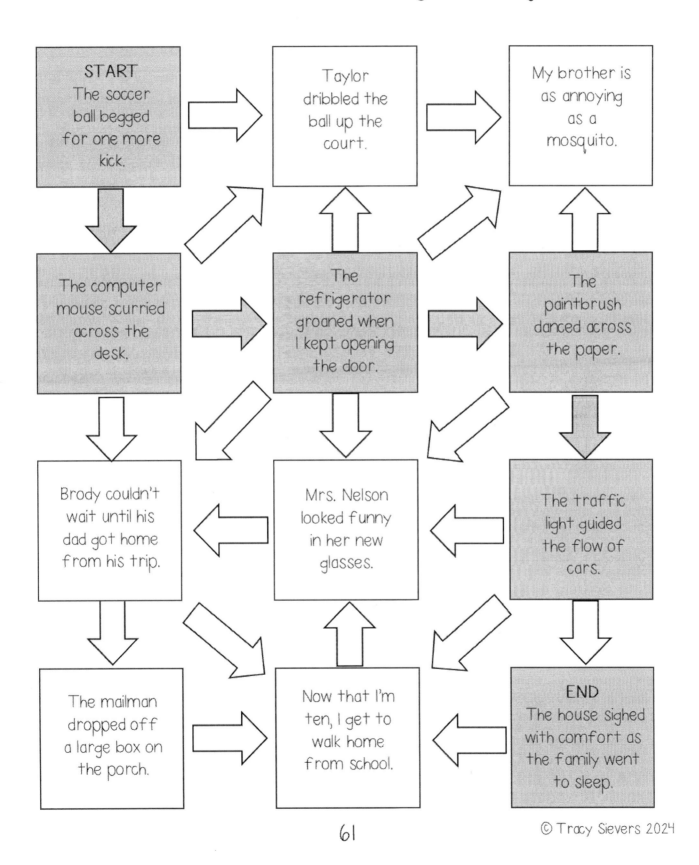

START
The soccer ball begged for one more kick.

Taylor dribbled the ball up the court.

My brother is as annoying as a mosquito.

The computer mouse scurried across the desk.

The refrigerator groaned when I kept opening the door.

The paintbrush danced across the paper.

Brody couldn't wait until his dad got home from his trip.

Mrs. Nelson looked funny in her new glasses.

The traffic light guided the flow of cars.

The mailman dropped off a large box on the porch.

Now that I'm ten, I get to walk home from school.

END
The house sighed with comfort as the family went to sleep.

61

Spot the Onomatopoeia *Answer Key*

1. The tires screech as the car comes to a sudden stop.

2. The duck quacks loudly by the pond, chatting with its feathered friends.

3. Every time someone walks by, my dog barks loudly.

4. The scent of popcorn fills the room as it pops in the microwave.

5. As I step on the ice, I hear it crack beneath my feet.

6. The pig oinks happily in the mud, enjoying its bath.

7. The colorful leaves rustle in the gentle breeze.

8. I was woken up to the thud of my brother slamming his door.

9. The hum of the fan helped me drift off to sleep.

10. The ice cubes clink in the glass as Crista pours the soda.

Find Your Path Answer Key

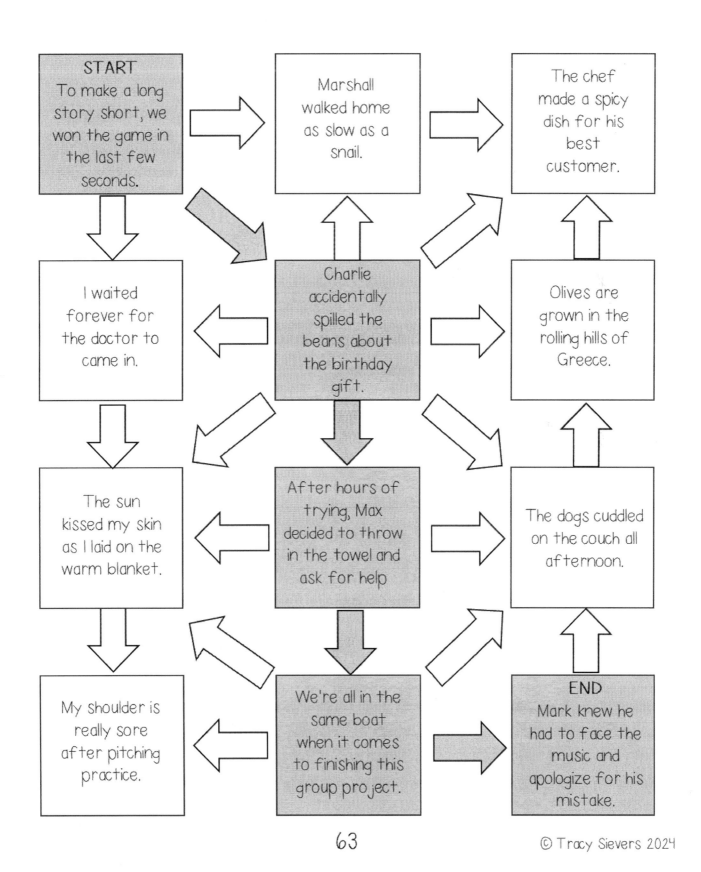

START
To make a long story short, we won the game in the last few seconds.

Marshall walked home as slow as a snail.

The chef made a spicy dish for his best customer.

I waited forever for the doctor to came in.

Charlie accidentally spilled the beans about the birthday gift.

Olives are grown in the rolling hills of Greece.

The sun kissed my skin as I laid on the warm blanket.

After hours of trying, Max decided to throw in the towel and ask for help

The dogs cuddled on the couch all afternoon.

My shoulder is really sore after pitching practice.

We're all in the same boat when it comes to finishing this group project.

END
Mark knew he had to face the music and apologize for his mistake.

Fill In Fun *Answer Key*

Word Bank				
wisdom	kite	tiptoed	children	Natalie
monkey	diary	battled	pink	scampered

1. Beneath the big, bustling bridge, bugs battled for bits of bread.

2. Katie the kind-hearted kid kept a keen eye on her kite.

3. Wally the wizard waved his wand, whispering words of wisdom to a wandering wolf.

4. Cheery children chased chubby chipmunks, chuckling in the cherry orchard.

5. Natalie noticed noisy neighborhood birds nesting near her new nectarine tree.

6. Silly squirrels scampered swiftly, searching for snacks.

7. Molly the mischievous monkey made marvelous mud pies.

8. Penny the pirate painted pictures of pink parrots and pirate ships.

9. Dr. Doodle drew dazzling dragons in his dusty old diary.

10. Terrific tigers tiptoed through the tangled trees.

Find Your Path *Answer Key*

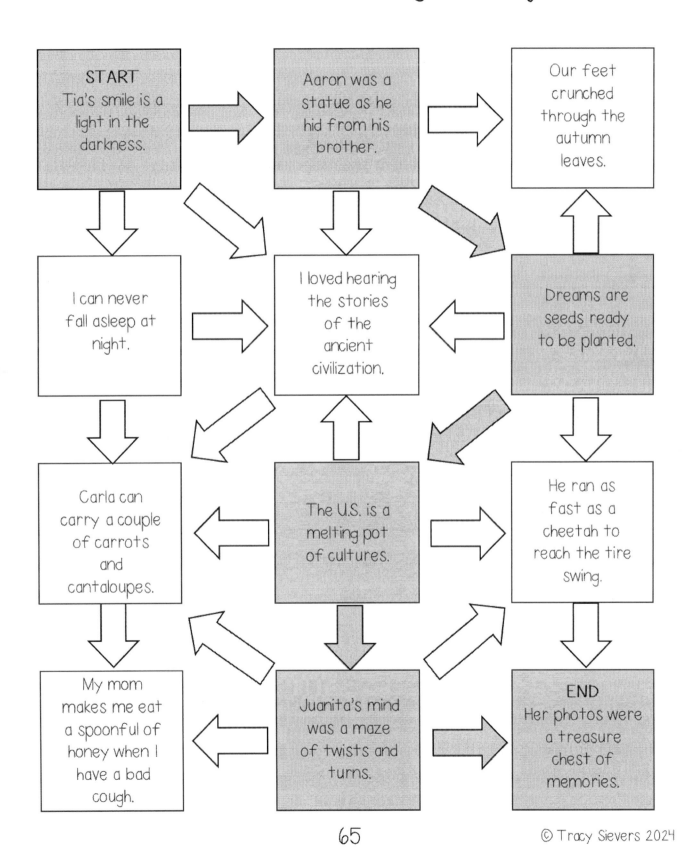

START
Tia's smile is a light in the darkness.

Aaron was a statue as he hid from his brother.

Our feet crunched through the autumn leaves.

I can never fall asleep at night.

I loved hearing the stories of the ancient civilization.

Dreams are seeds ready to be planted.

Carla can carry a couple of carrots and cantaloupes.

The U.S. is a melting pot of cultures.

He ran as fast as a cheetah to reach the tire swing.

My mom makes me eat a spoonful of honey when I have a bad cough.

Juanita's mind was a maze of twists and turns.

END
Her photos were a treasure chest of memories.

65

Fill In Fun Answer Key

arms	walked	page	groaned	ink
clock	road	hugged	clouds	wind

1. The wind whispered secrets through the trees.

2. The pencil raced across the page, eager to tell a story.

3. The stairs groaned under our weight

4. The shadows chased us as we walked.

5. The clock screamed at us to wake up.

6. The tree branches reached out like welcoming arms.

7. The clouds played hide and seek with the sun.

8. The dirt road stretched out before us.

9. The pen refused to cooperate, running out of ink.

10. The blanket hugged us to keep us warm.

Spot the Simile *Answer Key*

1. Deanna's eyes sparkled like diamonds in the early morning sunlight.

2. The raindrops fell from the sky like tiny dancers leaping across the stage.

3. Mr. Cane's voice was as loud as thunder during a storm.

4. The bird's song was as sweet as a lullaby.

5. The mountain stood tall and strong like a giant.

6. The baby's cheeks were as pink as cotton candy.

7. The flowers in the garden bloomed like colorful fireworks.

8. The snowflakes fell from the sky as gently as feathers.

9. Ann's blonde hair flowed behind her like a golden river.

10. The rainbow stretched across the sky like a colorful bridge.

Find Your Path Answer Key

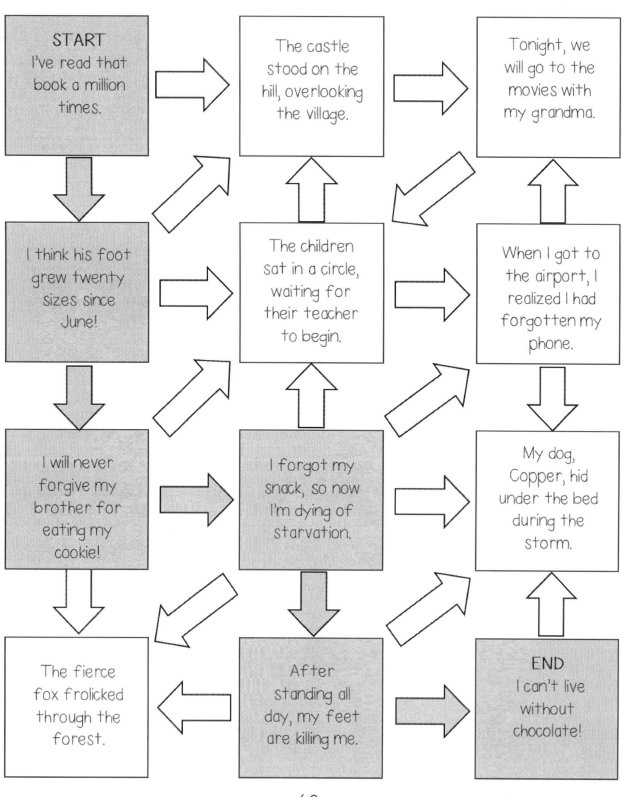

START
I've read that book a million times.

The castle stood on the hill, overlooking the village.

Tonight, we will go to the movies with my grandma.

I think his foot grew twenty sizes since June!

The children sat in a circle, waiting for their teacher to begin.

When I got to the airport, I realized I had forgotten my phone.

I will never forgive my brother for eating my cookie!

I forgot my snack, so now I'm dying of starvation.

My dog, Copper, hid under the bed during the storm.

The fierce fox frolicked through the forest.

After standing all day, my feet are killing me.

END
I can't live without chocolate!

Spot the Personification *Answer Key*

1. The backpack slouched under the weight of the books.

2. The haunted house patiently waited for the children to enter.

3. The stars winked at us from the night sky.

4. The leaves waved goodbye as they fell from the trees.

5. As the river flowed, it sang a gentle lullaby.

6. The thunder growled angrily in the distance.

7. The flashlight guarded us in the darkness.

8. The recess whistle demanded the attention of the students.

9. The gooey pizza called out to be eaten.

10. The roller coaster screamed as it came to a stop.

Fill In Fun *Answer Key*

Word Bank				
hit	ice	bag	biting	pigs
cake	around	nail	raining	bucket

1. That test was a piece of cake!

2. Making a joke helped me break the ice with my new classmates.

3. Sarah really hit the nail on the head when she guessed my favorite color.

4. Don't let the cat out of the bag about the surprise party!

5. My mom said I could get a pony for my birthday when pigs fly.

6. I wanted to join the soccer team, but I'm so busy that I might be biting off more than I can chew.

7. It's not just a light drizzle, it's raining cats and dogs out there!

8. Stop beating around the bush and just tell me what happened.

9. I hope to travel the world before I kick the bucket

10. After a long day, I'm ready to hit the hay.

Find Your Path *Answer Key*

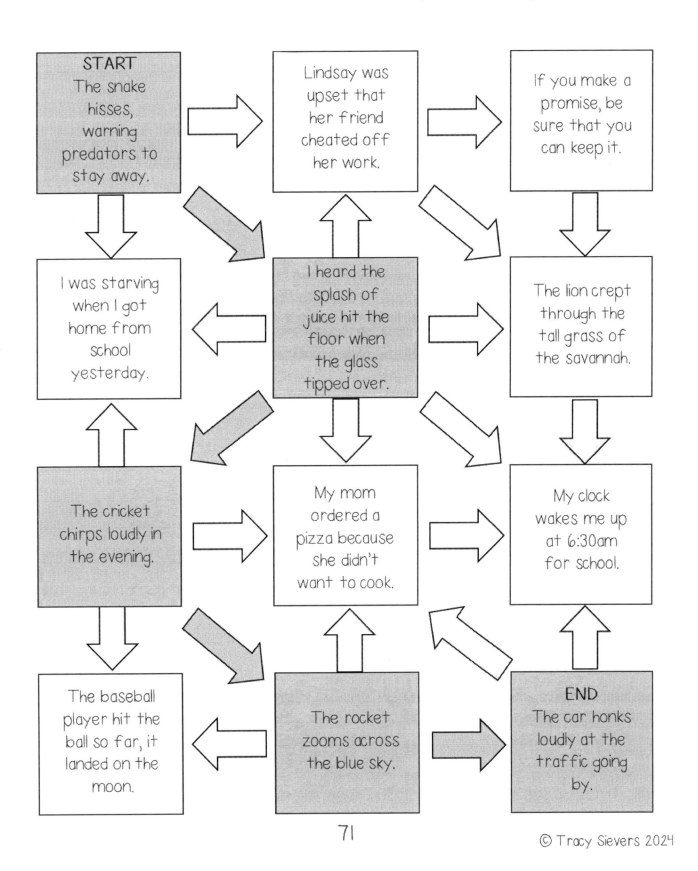

Fill In Fun *Answer Key*

Word Bank				
zoomed	popped	wand	bird	curiosity
air	honey	twinkled	slithering	tears

1. Her tears fell like silent raindrops on a windowpane.

2. The silence hung in the air like a heavy cloud.

3. His curiosity bubbled up inside him like a fizzy soda

4. The basketball player soared through the air like a bird taking flight.

5. The campfire crackled and popped like a bowl of popcorn

6. The stars twinkled above like a host of fireflies in the night sky.

7. The car zoomed down the road as fast as a shooting star.

8. The paintbrush danced across the canvas like a magician's wand.

9. The roller coaster twisted and turned like a snake slithering through the air.

10. The cookie was as sweet as honey dripping from a hive.

Fill In Fun *Answer Key*

Word Bank				
crackles	hooves	rumbles	clock	whooshes
pan	buzz	meows	birds	rain

1. The bees buzz around the flowers, gathering nectar.

2. The tick tock of the clock counts down the minutes until recess.

3. The thunder rumbles loudly, like a giant's belly at dinnertime.

4. The rain pitter-patters on the roof, making it hard to hear what my mom is saying.

5. The horse's hooves clippity-clop along the cobblestone street.

6. The fire crackles in the fireplace as we snuggle on the couch.

7. The cat meows loudly outside the door when he wants to come in.

8. The birds chirp cheerfully in the morning, singing a wake-up song.

9. The wind whooshes through the trees, like a superhero rushing by.

10. The pan sizzles as the bacon cooks in the skillet.

Spot the Alliteration Answer Key

1. Fiona the fearless fairy flew through the forest, fluttering her feathery wings.

2. Gabe and Greta gobbled yummy gummy bears.

3. Hannah happily hummed her favorite tunes while hiking through the heavenly hills.

4. In July, Jake and Jenny joyfully drove to the jamboree.

5. Little Lucy listened to the lullabies of the lazy, lapping waves.

6. Ruby the rabbit raced rapidly around the wet, rocky road.

7. Swiftly sliding down snowy slopes, round snowmen sang silly songs .

8. Curious cats cuddled together, watching the colorful caterpillars .

9. Daring Danny delightfully darted down the orange slide.

10. Busy bees buzzed in the budding blossoms.

Find Your Path Answer Key

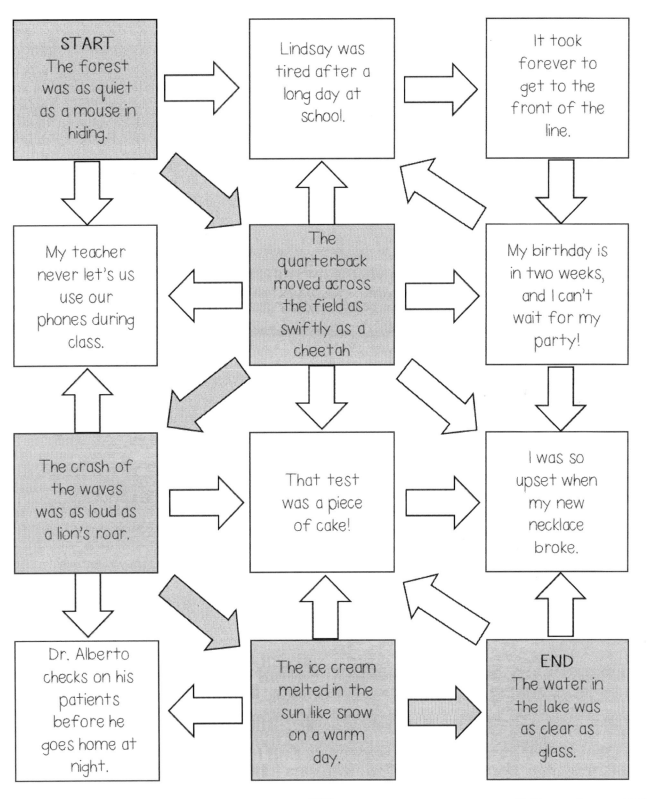

START
The forest was as quiet as a mouse in hiding.

Lindsay was tired after a long day at school.

It took forever to get to the front of the line.

My teacher never let's us use our phones during class.

The quarterback moved across the field as swiftly as a cheetah

My birthday is in two weeks, and I can't wait for my party!

The crash of the waves was as loud as a lion's roar.

That test was a piece of cake!

I was so upset when my new necklace broke.

Dr. Alberto checks on his patients before he goes home at night.

The ice cream melted in the sun like snow on a warm day.

END
The water in the lake was as clear as glass.

75

Spot the Idiom Answer Key

1. Tell me all about your day, I'm all ears.

2. Don't worry about the test next week. Let's cross that bridge when we get to it.

3. Be sure to sign up for a few classes so you don't put all your eggs in one basket.

4. My grandma came to visit out of the blue.

5. Right before the Spelling Bee I had butterflies in my stomach.

6. Don't celebrate until the game is over because we don't want to count our chickens before they hatch.

7. I got my chores done by 9:00am because the early bird catches the worm.

8. There's no need to make a mountain out of a molehill.

9. The new girl hoped her classmates wouldn't judge a book by its cover.

10. When Sandra got caught in a lie, she found herself in a pickle.

Fill In Fun *Answer Key*

Word Bank				
wake	brain	lightning	skyscraper	homework
waited	universe	suitcase	sleep	million

1. Kaitlyn grew taller than a skyscraper last summer.

2. I've told you a million times to clean your room.

3. His snoring is so loud, it could wake the dead.

4. I can't carry my suitcase because it weighs a ton!

5. I'm so tired today, I could sleep for a week.

6. My grandma makes the best cookies in the entire universe.

7. I've got a mountain of homework to do tonight.

8. I'm pretty sure my brother's brain is the size of a pea.

9. I waited in line for ages to get tickets for the concert.

10. Nevaeh is faster than lightning on the basketball court.

Find Your Path *Answer Key*

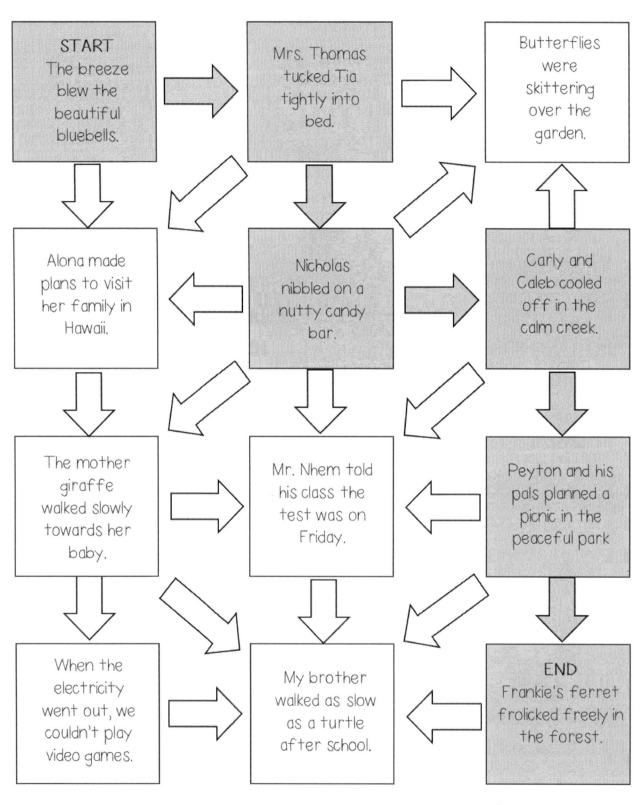

START
The breeze blew the beautiful bluebells.

Mrs. Thomas tucked Tia tightly into bed.

Butterflies were skittering over the garden.

Alona made plans to visit her family in Hawaii.

Nicholas nibbled on a nutty candy bar.

Carly and Caleb cooled off in the calm creek.

The mother giraffe walked slowly towards her baby.

Mr. Nhem told his class the test was on Friday.

Peyton and his pals planned a picnic in the peaceful park

When the electricity went out, we couldn't play video games.

My brother walked as slow as a turtle after school.

END
Frankie's ferret frolicked freely in the forest.

Spot the Metaphor *Answer Key*

1. The ocean is a giant, blue blanket stretching to the horizon.

2. Problems are puzzles, waiting to be solved.

3. The road to success is a winding path with many twists and turns.

4. Eva's dream was the spark that ignited her creativity.

5. Forgiveness is a bridge that mends broken hearts.

6. My brother is a squirrel, always scurrying around.

7. Chloe's smile is a ray of sunshine on a rainy day.

8. Mr. Wooten's words were a sword that cut through the silence.

9. The world is a playground full of adventures waiting to happen.

10. The moon is a silver coin in the dark sky.

Spot the Hyperbole Answer Key

1. I have a billion things on my mind right now.

2. My mom is blind without her glasses.

3. My backpack is bursting at the seams with books.

4. The party was louder than a rock concert.

5. I've been studying for hours and now my brain is mushy.

6. The traffic jam was so long that I thought I'd never get home.

7. The price of gas is sky-high!

8. My mom's to-do list is never-ending.

9. I have looked everywhere for my keys.

10. Knox was so hungry, he felt like he could eat fifty cheeseburgers.

BONUS: Pick the Personification Answer Key

1. The mischievous wind gently (danced/blew) through the trees.

2. The sun (shone/smiled) down on the playground, warming the swings and slides.

3. The car engine (coughed/sputtered) as it struggled to start on the chilly morning.

4. The blanket snugly (hugged/wrapped around) Amanda, keeping her warm at her brother's football game.

5. The clock on the wall (ticked away/counted down) the seconds until recess would start.

6. The floor of the old house (groaned/creaked) as the family walked down the hall.

7. The stars (sparkled/winked) in the sky as we laid in the grass.

8. The thunder crashed (angrily/loudly), shaking the earth..

9. As we sat at the campsite, the moon (glowed/peeked out) from behind the clouds.

10. The raindrops (fell/tap-danced) on the roof of the school.

BONUS: Onomatopoeia Matching *Answer Key*

flutter — wings
tick tock — clock
vroom — engine
zap — electricity
clink — ice cubes in a glass
beep — car horn
crash — cymbals
boom — fireworks
hiss — snake
sizzle — bacon
whoosh — wind
buzz — bee
drip — water

BONUS: Match the Hyperbole *Answer Key*

1. I waited forever for my turn. **G**

2. My backpack weighed a ton! **H**

3. My teacher gave us ten hours of homework. **F**

4. We ran a marathon on P.E. **I**

5. I'm starving! I could eat an elephant. **E**

6. It was so cold outside that my toes froze on my walk home. **C**

7. My dog runs faster than a fighter jet. **A**

8. I was too nervous to go down the waterslide because it was taller than a skyscraper. **J**

9. I'm so tired I could sleep for a hundred years. **B**

10. After working on our project, it looked like a tornado hit our classroom. **D**

A. he's fast

B. I'm really sleepy

C. the temperature was low

D. it was messy

E. I'm very hungry

F. I had a lot to do

G. the wait was long

H. it was heavy

I. we ran a long distance

J. it was very tall

Name It! Answer Key

1. After the long soccer game, Joy's legs felt as heavy as lead weights.

1. simile

2. The thunderstorm boomed and rumbled overhead, making me jump with each loud clap.

2. onomatopoeia

3. The heavy backpack was an anchor, weighing down Leroy's shoulders as he trudged home from school.

3. metaphor

4. Jenna was so excited for her birthday party that she was on cloud nine all week.

4. idiom

5. The fluffy white clouds in the sky looked as soft as cotton balls.

5. simile

6. Sahir's sweet, sticky syrup spread slowly over his stack of pancakes.

6. alliteration

7. Lily was a shining star on the dance floor, her movements graceful and mesmerizing.

7. metaphor

8. Mom gave me a million reminders to clean my room.

8. hyperbole

9. The chocolate cake winked at me from the kitchen counter, tempting me with its rich frosting.

9. personification

10. Furry forest friends frolicked through the fallen fall leaves.

10. alliteration

Fill In Fun 2.0 Answer Key

Answers will vary.

simile
1. The baby's scream was as loud as a fire alarm

metaphor
2. The night sky was a string of lanterns, twinkling down on the valley.

hyperbole
3. This backpack weighs a ton!

personification
4. The raindrops danced in the puddles, splashing in the afternoon sun.

alliteration
5. The bouncy, black ball bobbed across Ben's bright blue bedroom.

onomatopoeia
6. The puppy's tail thumped excitedly against the floor when I gave him a treat.

idiom
7. After hours of begging, mom finally gave Lucy the green light to have a sleepover.

simile
8. The ice cream sundae was as tall as a mountain with scoops of ice cream and toppings piled high.

metaphor
9. The math test was a puzzle that Jake struggled to solve.

hyperbole
10. My dad's snoring could have woken the neighbors last night.

personification
11. The old truck groaned with effort as it climbed the steep hill.

alliteration
12. Crispy, crunchy carrots crackled between Chloe's teeth.

onomatopoeia
13. The bees buzzed busily as they gathered nectar from the colorful flowers.

Idiom
14. After a terrible tryout, Jameson felt like he had two left feet when it came to soccer.

Figurative Facts *Answer Key*

1. Hyperboles must be realistic descriptions.

1. False

2. Figurative language can be used to make writing more interesting.

2. True

3. Onomatopoeia is when words imitate the sounds they describe.

3. True

4. A simile uses "like" or "as" to compare two things.

4. True

5. You must use a letter ten times in a sentence for it to be considered alliteration.

5. False

6. Idioms would be difficult to understand if English wasn't your first language.

6. True

7. Hyperboles can make things sound bigger or smaller than they really are.

7. True

8. Personification gives human traits to non-human things.

8. True

9. You can only use onomatopoeia for animal sounds.

9. False

10. Similes and metaphors are the same thing.

10. False

THANK YOU!

Hey y'all! I'm Tracy... I spent 21 years in an elementary classroom in Texas. I began as a first grade teacher and then moved to a talent and gifted specialist for grades K-5. The last years of my career were spent in fifth grade. I then decided to trade in my recess whistle and felt tip pens to spend my days writing curriculum and creating literacy resources for YOU!

Thank you for purchasing this resource! I hope you love it as much as I do. I take great pride in making teachers' lives easier AND making learning fun.

CREDITS

https://www.teacherspayteachers.com/Store/Kaitlynn-Albani

https://www.teacherspayteachers.com/Store/Biddys-Math-Binder

https://www.teacherspayteachers.com/Store/Lindsay-Bowden-Secondary-Math

88

LET'S KEEP IN TOUCH!

https://www.instagram.com/raiseyourhandresources/

https://www.teacherspayteachers.com/Store/Tracy-Sievers-Raise-Your-Hand-Resources

https://raise-your-hand-resources.ck.page/f7022779e1

Made in United States
Orlando, FL
20 October 2024

52945646R00050